Leadership

Essential Abilities Needed To Develop Into A Formidable Female Leader, Meet The Obstacles Posed By Contemporary Company And The Workplace, And Guide Productive Teams And Instill Motivation In Your Staff

Lonnie Allison

TABLE OF CONTENT

Have Joy And Abundance In Your Spiritual Life 1

"I Perceive A Transition Approaching," Stated Ryan 19

Demonstrate Some Of That Competitive Energy. 46

What Does It Mean To Lead? 114

The Innovative Front-Runner 127

Baby Boomers And Members Of Generation Y Are Separated By A Generational Divide. 140

Have Joy And Abundance In Your Spiritual Life

A considerable number of individuals tend to disregard the subject of spiritual life unless they actively engage in a particular form of spiritual practice. However, it must be acknowledged that one's spiritual beliefs hold significant value in determining their overall success. It is imperative to have a firm grounding in one's spirituality, regardless of one's chosen faith, as it may prove challenging to attain the desired level of success without this essential element in place. In this chapter, we examine several aspects pertaining to one's spiritual well-being, which can contribute significantly to long-term success.

Meditation

Engaging in meditative practice bears advantages for one's well-being. Meditative practices involve techniques that aid in focusing and directing one's concentration and thoughts towards a specific focal point on a regular basis. Meditation also entails an introspective contemplation or focused attention on a specific sensation or concept. A multitude of religious traditions have an extensive historical background of employing contemplative techniques to cultivate empathy, benevolence, and mindfulness, as well as to pacify the mind.

Engaging in contemplation can evoke feelings of tranquility and mental clarity, alongside enhancing one's ability to concentrate and deliberate. Researchers in the field of neuroscience have extensively investigated these concepts, with a significant body of evidence indicating that the practice of contemplation leads to structural changes in the brain, resulting in a reduced sensitivity to pain, an enhanced immune system, improved emotional regulation, and alleviation of stress. Careful contemplation has been shown to be beneficial for individuals suffering from cancer, anxiety and depression, chronic pain, fibromyalgia, rheumatoid arthritis, type 2 diabetes, and cardiovascular conditions.

Invocation towards a divine entity can evoke a cathartic response, accompanied by sentiments of faith, gratitude, and compassion, all of which contribute positively to overall welfare. In various forms, individuals make entreaties to a divine being, most of which are grounded in the belief in a higher power that exerts influence upon one's existence. This conviction can provide a sense of consolation and support during challenging circumstances. A research study revealed that adult individuals diagnosed with clinical depression exhibited significantly better response to medication when they held the belief that their prayers were acknowledged by a divine entity, as compared to those who did not hold such a belief.

Yoga is an ancient discipline that entails cultivating a sense of unity within the practitioner through the implementation of physical postures, ethical practices, and breath expansion. The proficient application of yoga has been demonstrated to mitigate irritability and anxiety, alleviate depression and unease, decrease blood pressure, and enhance overall feelings of well-being.

Journaling is an alternative meditation practice that is often overlooked, yet it offers a valuable avenue for increasing self-awareness and fostering a greater sense of interconnectedness with one's inner world and the surrounding environment. Research suggests that engaging in reflective writing during challenging periods can facilitate the exploration of personal meaning in life's adversities and promote resilience, even in the face of adversity.

The concept of the democratic approach has been previously explored and once more underscores the importance of achieving consensus through active participation.

The authoritative approach can be deemed comparable to the autocratic leadership style highlighted earlier.

There exist four additional leadership styles that have been defined, with a heightened emphasis on leadership in contemporary society.

Transactional leadership places its attention on the operational aspects and activities undertaken on a daily basis. This leader faces difficulties in perceiving an overarching strategy or effectively communicating their vision. Transactional leaders place a strong emphasis on an individual's assigned duties and obligations. They implement assertive strategies to manage the performance of team members who fail to meet expectations, thereby resulting in diminished morale.

Transformational leadership serves as a platform for fostering innovation within an organization by means of inspiring and motivating the team. These leaders are committed to elevating their organizations by effectively leading teams that exhibit exceptional performance and engagement. This leadership is attained by means of effective communication, articulation of vision, upholding integrity, exhibiting emotional intelligence, demonstrating authenticity, and displaying self-awareness. This particular style is widely recognized as prevalent in the business field.

Charismatic leadership comprises the elements of transformational leadership through the means of inspiring and motivating others. Nevertheless, the leader stands to gain from this. This leader lacks a strong dedication towards fostering innovation and driving the organization towards excellence. This particular approach frequently culminates in the downfall of numerous establishments.

Servant leadership was initially delineated in 1970 by Robert Greenleaf, who characterized it as an innate inclination to lead through acts of service, seeking to fulfill the needs of team members, granting them decision-making authority, fostering their development, and ensuring the satisfaction of their fundamental requirements.

Frequently, the servant-leader does not receive formal acknowledgement. The leader often remains unrecognized and directs attention towards the accomplishments of the individual members of the team.

The advantages of adopting servant leadership encompass elevated levels of engagement, thereby culminating in enhanced team performance. The team members experience a sense of validation and exhibit heightened levels of involvement. They perceive that the leader demonstrates genuine concern for their welfare and overall welfare.

The team exhibits elevated levels of morale by adhering to a strong ethical framework. This individual demonstrates exemplary leadership qualities, exemplifying unwavering integrity, placing equal emphasis on the welfare of both the organization and its team members, prioritizing the interests of various stakeholders, and displaying exceptional self-awareness.

There exist foundational competencies of servant leadership that are applicable across various leadership styles. In the subsequent sections of this book, you shall acquire an understanding of these fundamental principles and their appropriate implementation.

In order to be successful in a leadership role, it is essential to possess an understanding of which style of leadership to employ. Recognizing the importance of utilizing different styles based on the specific circumstances and the context of one's leadership role.

It is now opportune to reflect upon oneself in the mirror, aiming to enrich one's self-awareness.

Unidentified Influencers

As I engaged in meaningful dialogue with the executive leadership team of the organization and immersed myself in the workings of the enterprise, I gradually discerned the previously unacknowledged individuals who held considerable sway over its affairs, hereafter referred to as the "unidentified influencers" (UIs) of the business. I was highly impressed by Zack's expertise in the technical facets of the industry, his extensive experience within the field, and his discerning understanding of areas where the organizational culture could be enhanced during our initial encounter on the night shift. Zack also played an active role in the business's safety team, and his peers exhibited and conveyed their high regard for him through various nonverbal cues displayed in his presence. On the contrary, during my engagement with several managers within the company, Zack's name was frequently brought up accompanied by expressions of frustration. Managers may legitimately harbor frustration towards certain employees, but I have observed that most instances of long-standing "frustrating employees" are a direct consequence of managers being pushed and tested by said employees. It was evident to me that Zack possessed a sense of proprietorship over the enterprise; nevertheless, he experienced dissatisfaction due to the deficient execution and monitoring of significant matters and prospects within the organization.

While investigating the identities of the user interfaces within the company, I was approached by a team from one of the nighttime shifts (given that the organization maintained round-the-clock operations with four 12-hour shifts spanning three to four days a week, followed by a one-week break every other month). This team approached me subsequent to my initial introductory town hall in order to dispute one of the key points I made during my introduction. I typically inquire about "the individuals who had intended to come to work that day with the intention of committing mistakes, deviating from standard procedures, or causing an accident" and, as expected, no one raises their hand in response. However, the purpose of this query is to create a relaxed atmosphere and emphasize that individuals do not come to work with the intention to fail or make errors. This team extended an invitation for me to join them during one of the evenings allotted for their work. They wished to demonstrate to me the course of a notable mistake that had occurred during their duty, leading to disciplinary admonitions for two operators due to the adverse consequences on the product batch (each batch produced at the facility held considerable financial worth and was crucial for our clients in supplying medicine to their patients). Upon the conclusion of the town hall meeting, I politely inquired if it would be possible for us to promptly commence the examination of the described situation. They consented and requested a 30-minute period to assemble the pertinent documents that they wished to review in my presence.

Upon convening in the conference room thirty minutes thereafter, the table was adorned with the consequential documentation pertaining to a batch manufactured for a biological drug substance. They identified three distinct segments of the batch record and requested that I peruse the initial one. While perusing the guidelines outlined in the batch record pertaining to a particular stage of the process, I encountered numerous inquiries arising from a comprehensive examination aimed at ensuring comprehension. Upon completion of reading this particular segment of the batch record, I was subsequently guided to a designated set of instructions and prompted regarding the measures I would take to comply with said directives. Upon admitting my deficiency in practical involvement in biologics drug substance manufacturing, I proceeded to outline the reasoned steps I would undertake in adherence to the given guidance. The team responded with amusement and a sprinkling of sarcastic remarks. I discerned that I had been orchestrated, and now the anticipated juncture they intended to orchestrate for me had arrived.

The team's spokesperson expressed, "Engaging in such actions would result in a written disciplinary report, as it caused a deviation that had negative implications for the batch." Additionally, the remaining sections of the batch record that were indicated also contributed to the deviation, as they were subsequent errors directly linked to the initial decision labeled as an "operator error." The spokesperson subsequently commented, "As you correctly pointed out during the Town Hall meeting, our intention is not to intentionally make mistakes while performing our duties, but rather, the tools at our disposal inadvertently give rise to these errors. We have consistently communicated to our supervisor and manager the urgent need for input in the batch-record writing process to ensure an informed perspective." We have been informed that our contributions are considered invalid due to the greater expertise and capability of the technical writers in the technical services group, alongside the clients' endorsement of the batch records. We have requested the chance to conduct preliminary trials with the batch records prior to implementing them live, as we have done previously. Regrettably, the finalization of batch records occurs at the eleventh hour and the management exhibits an unwillingness to authorize an additional shift in order to guarantee the accuracy of batch records from the outset. Insufficient involvement from operational sources often results in the occurrence of these errors. As a consequence, operators are reprimanded for erroneously interpreting or inadequately comprehending ambiguous instructions.

I requested the team to grant me a brief period of time to conduct a thorough investigation into various matters.

What measures can be implemented to conduct a thorough examination of batch records prior to their execution?

In what manner can we enhance the clarity and precision of the batch record instructions, thereby mitigating any potential ambiguity or confusion?

Could there be any additional undisclosed information pertaining to the disciplinary action that the team may have withheld from me?

The team agreed with this timing, as this night was their last one for the week. I informed them that I would revert to them the subsequent week. As I proceeded to distance myself from the group and contemplated upon the events of the day and this particular circumstance, I found myself filled with a sense of enthusiasm. Drawing from previous encounters, I discerned that certain individuals within the team harbored the expectation that I would honor my commitment to further engage with them. Additionally, I was aware that there were other individuals within the team who were positioning themselves to reiterate their previous warnings in the event that I did not uphold my promise to them. I anticipated that this particular instance would serve as an early demonstration of positive transformation and the reestablishment of interdepartmental cohesion that had developed over time. I was eagerly looking forward to commencing the task.

"I Perceive A Transition Approaching," Stated Ryan.

Recall our previous conversation regarding the parallel between the necessity for the human body to engage all its muscle groups and the imperative for a company to actively engage its three fundamental muscle groups. Having previously deliberated on individuals and society, the focus of this evening's discussion will be directed towards the concept of progression. Yes, I am of the opinion that utilizing cigar making as an analogy would be a viable starting point. Initially, let us consider solely the discussion of manually-crafted cigars. Handcrafted cigars are composed entirely of pure tobacco, resulting in a superior aroma and flavor compared to commercially produced cigars.

Due to the manner in which artisanal cigars are crafted, it facilitates the production of innumerable flavors and textures based on the origin of the tobacco. Nevertheless, the complete procedure necessitates the involvement of numerous individuals. Throughout the entire process, commencing with the sowing of tobacco seeds, proceeding with the transference of young saplings to the fields, followed by fermentation, destemming operations, and culminating in the art of rolling, numerous individuals contribute their efforts. It constitutes a sequence of procedures that require strict regulation. Put simply, they are required to have foreseeable results.

Cigar enthusiasts rely on that consistency. Should they experience dissatisfaction at any point, it may result in the loss of a customer. I conjecture that these purveyors of cigars demonstrate discernment in their recruitment process, employing individuals who possess a genuine affection for cigars, investing considerable efforts in training them proficiently, and fostering a cohesive community ethos, thereby contributing to a reduced rate of employee turnover. Moreover, it is probable that they have implemented manifold measures or procedures aimed at ensuring that the series of operations are effectively accomplishing their intended goals. Considering the tangible characteristics of the product, it is my assumption that there would be a requirement for corresponding physical examinations or assessments. Next on our agenda, we must delve into these procedures.

Ah. I see. In principle, the process of manufacturing cigars bears resemblance to that of our veterinary compound pharmacy. Furthermore, we offer a tangible product that requires precise and consistent blending. A high level of predictability is crucial due to the potential harm or fatality that could be inflicted upon an animal with an improper blend. If this information were to circulate, our susceptibility to losing a considerable number of customers would substantially increase. There is a possibility that our reputation may be jeopardized.

Indeed, prior to the implementation of sustainable business processes, it is imperative to establish a comprehensive control framework. Based on my personal observations, a strong control framework can be attributed to four fundamental elements:

• A dedication to upholding integrity and ethical principles, • A strong adherence to values of integrity and ethics, • A steadfast commitment to moral values and principles, • A resolute dedication to maintaining integrity and ethical standards, • The unwavering commitment to upholding moral and ethical values,

"• a distinct delineation of authority," • a explicit allocation of authority, • a well-defined assignment of authority, • a transparent grant of authority, • a precise delegation of authority, • a comprehensive apportionment of authority, • a explicit transfer of authority, • a concise assignment of authority, • a definitive allotment of authority.

• A well-defined Policy on Policies that outlines all the specific written policies and procedures mandated by the company,

• a framework designed to ensure individuals are held responsible for attaining the mutually agreed-upon goals. • a structure that enforces individual responsibility for achieving the predetermined aims. • a mechanism that ensures people are answerable for accomplishing the pre-established objectives. • a methodology that fosters individual accountability to the collectively determined targets.

Earlier today, a thorough discussion was conducted surrounding the topics of values and culture in the vicinity of the pool. The matters deliberated upon encompassed concepts such as integrity and respect. Nevertheless, the imperative to conduct oneself with integrity and adhere to ethical principles remains non-negotiable, irrespective of the fundamental values upheld by one's organization. These principles are integral to the integrity of the institution.

As an illustration, how would you handle a high-achieving individual within your organization who demonstrated a deficiency in ethical conduct, leading to the embezzlement of company funds? Regardless of the monetary amount involved, such actions would not only demonstrate a deficiency in honesty and integrity, but also constitute a clear violation of the law.

Providing Coaching and Mentoring

Delivering effective coaching is an indispensable responsibility of a leader. It is the process of guiding an individual towards improving his or her performance. It prioritizes current conduct over historical manifestations.

Although certain individuals hold the belief that coaching and teaching are synonymous, it is vital to acknowledge that these two approaches to learning diverge significantly. While instructing imparts fresh knowledge to the recipient, coaching simply steers the individual in the direction of acquiring necessary competencies. It operates under the assumption that the individual possesses existing knowledge on enhancing their abilities and simply requires guidance to discern the necessary steps.

In the field of Coaching, coaches are not deemed to be the subject matter authorities. They lack comprehensive solutions to enhance an individual's performance. The person possessing the knowledge in the specific field is the individual. Coaches primarily serve as facilitators, aiding individuals in tapping into their full capabilities.

Leaders also undertake a significant responsibility in the form of mentoring. This pertains to the facilitation of accelerated learning and human development. Mentors possess a high level of expertise in their respective field and collaborate with individuals to facilitate their growth and development into skilled practitioners. Leaders who provide mentorship to their teams engage in the following practices:

Instruct – In situations where a team member lacks the requisite knowledge or skill to effectively carry out a task or fulfill a responsibility, competent leaders possess the ability to impart the required training. They engage in the active exchange of information with the objective of facilitating optimal performance among the members of their team.

Promote - Acquiring new knowledge can often elicit feelings of stress. Leaders ensure that their colleagues receive ample support and encouragement to mitigate the effects of such stress. As newcomers may still be lacking in self-assurance, excellent leaders ensure to consistently offer affirmations of their progress. Additionally, they offer stair targets to ensure that novice learners realize the importance of not needing to attain master level proficiency immediately.

Nurture – Mentoring revolves around aiding individuals in their ongoing pursuit of self-improvement. Leaders ensure that the individuals they collaborate with receive supplementary assistance following the initial training. Instructing others in the methodology of a task necessitates continual vigilance until it is internalized as a customary practice.

Mentorship does not entail excessive control and oversight; rather, it involves extending assistance to individuals in order to enable their self-improvement.

This is indeed one of the paramount objectives of a leader - to ensure incessant growth and progress among the individuals they collaborate with.

Embracing the Excellence of Others: A Comparative Exploration

Allow us to consider the association between Saul and David. Following David's triumph over Goliath, Saul developed an admiration for him and extended an invitation for David to reside in his palace. The Biblical account recounts that Saul bestowed upon David a position of elevated authority within the army. Nevertheless, following this initial phase of admiration and affection, Saul experiences a profound sense of resentment towards David, undertaking every conceivable effort to exclude him from his presence. Let us examine the process by which that reversal was achieved. 1 Sam. 18:7-9 describes the root cause of the enmity between Saul and David. Following David's appointment as the designated protector of the Israelites bestowed by God, the citizens of Saul's realm hold David in higher esteem compared to Saul.

Consequently, the women engaged in song and dance, proclaiming, "Saul has triumphed over thousands, whereas David has vanquished tens of thousands." This declaration incensed Saul greatly, and he expressed his dissatisfaction by remarking, "They have attributed ten thousands to David, while I am only attributed thousands." "What further possessions or acquisitions can he possibly desire, except for the kingdom?" Henceforth, Saul regarded David with a scrutinizing gaze. 18:7-9).

Saul found it intolerable that David, a soldier whom he had appointed, was being bestowed with more acclaim and reverence than himself within his realm. This narrative dates back to ancient times. However, to what extent do we observe such occurrences in contemporary religious congregations and Christian institutions? How frequently do we encounter this phenomenon in various spheres of existence?

Allow us to examine the life and ministry of a different individual named Saul, specifically the Saul referenced in the New Testament and widely recognized as Paul. Each and every one of us is well aware of the significant impact he had on Christianity, particularly during the early development of the church. The inclusion of his epistles to the various Churches of his time played an integral role in shaping our New Testament. Upon examining the life and ministry of Paul, it becomes evident that the course of his ministry could have been markedly divergent were it not for the influential presence of an individual referred to as Barnabas. The initial introduction to Barnabas is found in Acts 4:36-37. His given name was Joseph, and the appellation of Barnabas was bestowed upon him by the Apostles. The moniker Barnabas holds the significance of denoting "Offspring of Exhortation."

He achieved something remarkable alongside Paul. Upon Paul's arrival in Jerusalem following his conversion, the apostles harbored lingering doubts concerning his credibility. In fact, as documented in Acts 9:26, the Bible elucidates that there existed a sense of fear among them towards his presence. Nowadays, a significant portion of individuals refrain from rallying behind a controversial figure until they are aware of the viewpoints held by influential individuals in their vicinity. In the event that an individual of questionable background, specifically involving a history of criminal behavior, expresses an interest in becoming a member of our Church and initiates interactions with more recent Church attendees, it is highly probable that said newer members would seek the guidance and perspectives of the church's established elders prior to making any formal commitments. Paul's standing among others deteriorated even further. He was attributed with the persecution and execution of Christians. The recollection of Stephen's brutal execution, with Paul as an eyewitness who approved of this inhumane act, remained vivid in the apostles' collective consciousness. Therefore, Paul encountered challenges in his quest for acceptance among the group of disciples.

This is the point at which Barnabas entered the picture. Barnabas assumed the risk of endorsing Paul and advocated on his behalf. He had faith in Paul's abilities even prior to the consensus. Barnabas conveyed his formal and explicit support for Paul's leadership abilities to other prominent individuals within the community. Due to the recommendation of Barnabas, Paul is granted acceptance by the apostles and the ecclesiastical community. However, Barnabas does not cease his affiliation with Paul at that point. Barnabas subsequently endeavors to collaborate with Paul in Antioch, subsequently obtaining his initial missionary venture alongside Paul. The rest is history.

Therefore, we observe divergent methodologies employed by King Saul and Barnabas in embracing, fostering, and making substantial contributions to the excellence of their peers. Saul held a deep disdain for it and developed a resentful disposition. Barnabas derived great pleasure from it and offered his full support. To which category do we pertain? It is a universal aspiration for all of us to be included within the esteemed category of Barnabas. However, it is possible that the divine intention is for us to earnestly assess the depths of our hearts and ascertain the veracity of our intentions. I am not implying that our capacity for compassion, generosity, charity, or assistance is lacking. We sure are. However, the essence of Servant Leadership lies not solely in providing assistance, but rather in purposefully dedicating oneself to the growth and development of others, with the ultimate goal of enabling those individuals to surpass one's own accomplishments. I am confident that each one of us can attest to the assistance we have extended to numerous individuals who have become part of our lives - including our domestic helpers, colleagues under our supervision, members of our community, and so on. However, how many among us can truly claim to have engaged in actions that have elevated others above our own selves?

It is evident that complete sharing of all aspects is not feasible: each industry can be viewed as a distinct entity, comparable to a separate family within a different sector. Consequently, it is unavoidable that diverse approaches to managing human resources may exist within these entities.

However, it is essential for the company to maintain consistent setup and adhere to core values, as any deviations would introduce unnecessary complexities.

Should an individual within a team consistently fulfill the requirements set by their immediate manager without ever being taken into account in discussions pertaining to incentives, rewards, or promotions, it is inevitable that their long-term motivation will diminish.

He would start perceiving that his manager is not receiving the deserved level of respect, and consequently feel inclined to disregard his instructions, exerting his own authority and adopting the conduct of those who receive consistent rewards.

These lines of thought represent natural conclusions; however, they are prone to causing misallocation of resources and the proliferation of unorthodox individuals within an organization.

There is no aspect more crucial to an asset than the demonstration of their manager advocating for them. When the justification for a cause is sound, it becomes imperative to actively pursue it. Occasionally, it may yield no results, however, it is imperative that we make an effort as relinquishing these delicate matters would signal their irrevocable demise.

A resource that has proven to be effective in accordance with your instructions deserves appropriate recognition. It is imperative to impart comprehension to him, employing verbal communication, financial incentives, along with advantageous prospects ... It is imperative to ascertain (through identifying the most optimal approaches in this particular situation) that he is traversing the correct path and should persist in his endeavors accordingly.

Engage in a discourse and advocate for matters of significance. If a fellow colleague has executed their responsibilities proficiently and in accordance with established protocols, advocate on their behalf until you have garnered the maximum output from their efforts.

By implication, you are effectively conveying a resolute message to your team, demonstrating your commitment to advocate on their behalf and strive for optimal outcomes.

At times, it may not suffice; however, the intention itself is unequivocally evident and will undoubtedly be valued by your employees.

Alternatively, if you have a tendency to easily surrender when faced with initial challenges or conflicts regarding these matters, it will result in diminishing respect and trust from your team, and subsequently, the management of your resources will become increasingly intricate.

Seven: Converting Conflict into a Platform for Growth

To effectively lead amidst opposition, one must perceive every instance of disagreement as a chance for development and growth.

The Hebrew Individual Who Would Govern Egypt.

Earlier today in our Sunday School session, we were engaged in an examination of the life of an individual named Joseph.

If one is acquainted with the narrative, Joseph was an individual whom God appointed to assume the role of a national leader. What truly distinguishes the narrative is the fact that the nation over which he would assume leadership was not his place of origin, and the journey he embarked upon to reach that destination was quite unconventional.

In his youth, his own siblings developed an intense animosity towards him, to the point where they harbored literal intentions of taking his life. But his older brother Reuben intervened and they sold him into slavery instead.

Joseph would not have willingly selected such an option.

That ultimately resulted in a favorable outcome. Joseph has assumed the responsibility of overseeing his master's affairs. Indeed, such was the extent of his trustworthiness that the manner in which he handled matters did not elicit any scrutiny.

Subsequently, amidst his master's wife's persistent advances in pursuing him for an illicit affair, Joseph consistently turned her down until a pivotal moment occurred. She firmly clutched his sleeve, imploring him to acquiesce to her request. Instead of surrendering, Joseph chooses to escape, relinquishing his coat as it remains firmly grasped within her hands.

She seizes the occasion to level allegations of attempted rape against Joseph. His master, furious at the thought of it, throws Joseph into prison.

And you believed your existence was laden with hardship.

Once more, this was not the option Joseph would have preferred.

Shortly after, Joseph assumes the responsibility of overseeing all the remaining inmates. Indeed, his leadership prowess is so remarkable that no one even contemplates the manner in which he manages affairs.

Subsequently, on a certain day, two high-ranking officials of the Pharaoh found themselves incarcerated in the same prison as Joseph. He inquires about their concerns and one of them proceeds to recount a disquieting dream they had. The benevolent providence of the divine bestows upon him a favorable construal. Subsequently, Joseph pleads with the authority to recollect his existence upon resuming his professional duties in order to secure his release from incarceration.

After a span of three years, the official recollects Joseph. Subsequently, he proceeds to decipher a dream that is causing distress to Pharaoh. He is greatly impressed, leading him to appoint Joseph as the supreme authority in Egypt, holding a position subordinate only to the Pharaoh.

Conflict is Inevitable

The narrative of Joseph serves to exemplify two profound verities.

Conflict is an inherent aspect of human existence, irrespective of personal preferences.

Despite meticulous life planning, it is highly conceivable that the outcome may deviate from the original intentions.

Today, we will explore how individuals can transform every instance of conflict into a valuable opportunity.

Decide What You Want

Motivational speakers advocate the importance of establishing objectives as a means to achieve desired outcomes in one's life.

One may employ a similar method in addressing conflicts.

Upon the occurrence of a conflict, what outcome do you desire? Shouldn't you establish a clear objective for triumph if you are inclined to participate in a potential altercation that may escalate into violence?

Regarding work, we partake in conflict due to three primary factors.

Demonstrate Some Of That Competitive Energy.

People who thrive in a competitive environment are the best candidates for leadership roles. If you are not typically competitive, you should make an effort to become so in order to build a reputation as someone who is willing to fight for what they believe to be right. Supervisors are eager to fill leadership roles with individuals whom they are confident will work hard to achieve the organization's objectives. In addition, followers are drawn to leaders who engage in healthy competition with one another because they believe such leaders have a greater chance of achieving their goals.

If at all possible, you should steer clear of direct competition in the business world. Putting into practice this strategy will enable you to keep your resources for the long haul. Having said that, there are instances in which you simply have to compete with other individuals or organizations. When you find yourself in a situation like this, you should be prepared to meet the challenge head on. You will need to acquire the ability to compete in order to achieve the organization's goals. You instill a sense of healthy competition in your followers by modeling this quality for them and encouraging them to emulate it themselves.

You will be able to give your followers a reason to continue being persistent if you generate a sense of competition among them. You will reawaken a competitive spirit within your followers and inspire them to take the lead. They will have something to look forward to each morning, which will motivate them to get out of bed and get to work.

If you want to demonstrate your competitive spirit, try to show that you are persistent in the actions you take to reach your goals. When you or your organization are up against tough competition, that is the best time to demonstrate your competitive spirit. For instance, the majority of people would give up trying to meet their sales quotas if they were living through difficult economic times. On the other hand, a competitive leader will always be on the lookout for new approaches that can help them achieve their goals.

It's possible the leader will make an effort to break into a new market. Additionally, he or she might make use of modern technology in order to expand the number of potential customers reached. Simply having a competitive spirit is not enough to guarantee that you will do well in the role of leader in your organization. Nevertheless, this goes a long way toward motivating your followers to continue working hard toward the goals of the organization they follow.

Maintain your standing among the people you associate with.

If people stop remembering you, you won't have a reputation to protect for very long. Effective leaders steer clear of this situation at all costs by ensuring they remain relevant within their respective communities. A great number of people look down on the concept of being the focus of attention. You should make an effort to accept this role in order to ensure that the people around you will always remember you.

You need to find a way to steal the spotlight without drawing attention to yourself. For instance, make an effort to make use of your skills and the unique qualities that you possess that other people lack. Utilize your conventionally attractive appearance, for instance, as a strength in your strategy to attract people's attention. You could also use fashion to highlight and emphasize the distinctive features of your appearance.

The Struggle for Honesty, Which Is the Most Important Quality in a Leader to Have in 8

As was covered in the previous chapter, two of the most important qualities a good leader should possess are struggle and honesty. In this chapter, we are going to talk about how perseverance through adversity and the strength that comes from being honest can transform a common man into a genuine leader.

It is advised that one should fight hard for the truth, even if it appears that the entire world is working against them in their efforts to achieve it. If you are confident that whatever it is you are doing is in service of uncovering the truth, then you should not be afraid to keep up the fight. In point of fact, nobody will be able to prevent you from carrying it out, and on the other hand, everyone will gradually begin to look up to you as a leader. Even if all of your money is wasted, but you still have the courage to fight for the truth, then people will look up to you as a leader rather than a common man. It is enough for a common man to take a stand for the truth and to be the person who is able to fight for the truth while maintaining his or her integrity. Your status as a leader will become more obvious as a result of this.

Participate in the fight for integrity and the truth. Don't let anything hold you back. If during the first half of the war people see you as the person who is willing to break social norms or barriers in order to fight for the truth, you will gradually become a leader by the time the second half of the war rolls around thanks to the leadership qualities you possess. You shouldn't be restrained in any way, not even if the moon and the sun turn against you and the entire world conspires against you. It is true because if you retreat even a little bit or allow yourself to become discouraged even for a split second, it will be much harder for you to face the threats.

Struggle, Struggle, and Struggle Some More – at least until you reach a point where you can give others a glimmer of optimism in their own lives. Continue to exert yourself to the fullest extent until then. The fight for the truth is an ongoing process, and only courageous leaders have the intestinal fortitude to bear the process of fighting for the sake of the rest of the world.

A person who fights for the cause of the struggle should have muscles as strong as iron and nerves as strong as steel. This will allow them to be a leader who fights for the cause. His thought processes don't waver, and he doesn't disconnect himself from the fight for the truth. A person who is incapable of fighting for the sake of the truth will simply be referred to as a common man because he does not possess the fundamental qualities of a leader.

During the fight for truth, many people are knocked down, and a great number of others even lose their lives. But none of these things should be allowed to derail the plans of a leader. Even if only one or two of them are able to win and make a comeback, the victory will be that of the truth. Throughout the entirety of the process, those individuals who demonstrate the desire to return are the ones who will be given the title of leader. Even though he went into the fight as just another member of the populace, the fact that he prevailed there will establish him as a genuine leader. Those who are willing to fight to the end for the sake of the truth and give their lives as a martyr are also considered to be leaders because they had the bravery to give their very last drop of blood in order to see the truth triumph. It is through experiences like these that an average man can rise to the level of a leader and emerge victorious.

People are rich in the truest sense of the word when they dedicate their time, energy, and resources to improving the lives of those who are disadvantaged, destitute, and in need. We can also look at the example of laborers, who will never be mentioned by name in the annals of human history despite the fact that it is these individuals who actually carry out the work. They might appear to the average person to be nothing more than simple laborers, but in reality, these are the people who are toiling away behind the scenes to make the world a better place for everyone. They are the ones who do the work, not the educated, regardless of whether or not they can read or write. They are the ones who take on the role of leaders while maintaining the appearance of a common man. If you are one of them or know any laborers, you need to keep in mind that they are also leaders in society, keeping in mind the contribution that they have made towards their society. If you do not do this, you will be forgetting an important fact.

A leader is someone who has a deep-seated passion for the truth and places the welfare of their followers as their top priority. A leader is someone who is just like the other people in the group but has the ability to inspire and motivate them. If you are not able to pass on the passion that burns in your heart to the hearts of your fellow soldiers or comrades, then you are not contributing anything positive. You cannot be considered a genuine leader.

The source of power for those who follow a leader is the leader themselves. When a regular guy uses his good qualities to exert influence over other people and succeeds, he begins to show signs of becoming a leader over time.

For a leader, showing weakness is equivalent to taking one's own life. Therefore, a leader ought to always be powerful. It is necessary that he be the most powerful of his allies. If he is not the strongest member of the group but he is still the leader, then his status as leader is a case of "mistaken identity." He is not capable of ever being a leader. On the other hand, a leader can come from any walk of life if he has the mental fortitude to do so. One has to come to terms with the fact that weakness can only lead to slavery and not leadership.

Please don't weep in the name of the Lord. Don't blame God for the things you just can't accomplish. If you are unable to do something, it indicates that you are lacking in some way. A leader is someone who can accept responsibility for their actions, regardless of whether they have won or lost. If the average person has the ability to accept responsibility for his actions, then he is the best possible leader, or at the very least, he possesses the qualities of a good leader. Those who place blame on God for things about which they have no knowledge are part of the common man population and can never be considered leaders. A person is considered to be a leader when they are able to accept responsibility for any outcome, whether it be a victory or a loss, without feeling any shame or guilt because they are confident that they gave their all along with their teammates. A leader must always be able to take a stand for the sake of the truth and be able to destroy anything that comes in the way of withholding justice.

A genuine leader is one who reveres power and the ability to win battles. A leader venerates strength because he is aware that it is only the strength of both body and soul that can assist him in prevailing over the challenges of life and the conflict against dishonesty in order to protect the general populace.

All of the aforementioned characteristics should be exhibited by a true leader. A common man must not only adhere to them in order to become a leader, but also follow the doctrines that prescribe how to be brave enough and become bold enough to save others. This is necessary for the common man to become a leader.

Conceptions that aren't true about Loyalty

There are some beliefs that people have about loyalty that are simply wrong, incorrect, or flawed, and they can lead to problems. These beliefs can be problematic. There are times when we define loyalty by specific behaviors that are not true signs of loyalty; rather, they are true signs of something else.

One of these is acting in a manner that is excessively subservient or almost servile. There are some leaders who like to surround themselves with people who will always say "yes," also known as "brown noses." They mistakenly believe that a sign of loyalty is having followers who agree with everything that they say; however, this is not the case. Someone who is loyal to you will tell you unpleasant news when you need to hear it, but these people won't do that for you.

The idea that a follower or worker will put all of their own self-interest and motivation to the side in order to concentrate on your well-being and self-interest as a priority rather than their own is a second flawed definition of loyalty. This is not the sign of someone you can trust; rather, it is the behavior of a slave or someone who lacks self-control. A trustworthy person would never behave in this manner.

You shouldn't be looking for this kind of loyalty; instead, you should try to find someone who will work with you to achieve your goals, rather than someone who will try to imitate your worldview at the expense of their own well-being. The concept that you have to have people who will follow you even when you give them bad advice is the best way that we can describe this flaw. It is the idea that you need to have blind obedience. You can tell everyone to drink the Kool-Aid or jump off the bridge, or you can have people take actions that are simply against their self-interest simply because of blind obedience. This is where we start moving down the path from loyalty into cultishness.

When people follow you and fall into alignment with you, you know that they are aware of your decision-making process and agree with you because loyalty comes with a certain measure of intelligence and active decision-making. In other words, they are intelligent enough to follow your lead. You can have checks and balances in your team in this way, so that if you are about to lead your team off a cliff, someone else will speak up and stop you before you all fall to your deaths. This is how you can ensure that your team is safe.

It's possible that you're thinking to yourself that this section is ridiculous and that no one would ever overly serve your team, but take a moment to examine how you act in certain situations. Have there been times in your life when your followers were too obedient, and you liked it just a little bit, or when you felt a little bit like a king? If so, tell me about those times. In the course of my life, I have encountered a few of those moments, and I believe that the vast majority of other people have, as well.

There are times when you need to check and analyze your own behavior to determine whether or not you are encouraging or requiring certain behaviors. Do you expect workers to report for duty on Saturdays, despite the fact that doing so strains their connections with their families? Do you require your employees to prioritize the needs of the company over those of their families? Because of this, the team will put in extra effort because they are in need of the money, but behind your back, they are all hoping that you will suffer an early heart attack. This is not the kind of group that you want to put together, and it is most definitely not the kind of group that I want to put together.

Know Yourself as a Leader "There is always a gap between the self we think we present, and the way others see us." This is the topic of 4, which is titled "Know Yourself as a Leader."

Sheila Heen and Douglas Stone, et al.

Figure Out Where Your Blind Spots Are

Blind spots are aspects of ourselves that we do not recognize, but which are obvious to others. The effort we put into getting to know ourselves better is directly correlated to the magnitude of our personal breakthroughs and advancements in leadership. On the other hand, our insecurities and shortcomings, also known as our blind spots, can be a barrier to our achievement. Here are some examples of the questions regarding feedback that you could ask:

What do you consider to be some of my best qualities?

What do you consider to be some of my flaws?

When I'm not around, what do you think other people talk about when it comes to me?

The moment you realized that other people view you as unapproachable was a monumental turning point. You don't intend to come across as unapproachable at all. You have the desire to connect with other people and to be accepted by them. You are aware that the desire you expressed does not match the expression on your face. Because you are now aware of this fact about yourself, you are going to pay closer attention to your facial expressions and make an effort to smile, make eye contact, and acknowledge other people. You also tell your friends and coworkers that this is your default face and that they should not read anything into it. Understanding this blind spot enables you to see yourself in the world and behave in a manner that is congruent with your goals. You, too, can gain an understanding of your blind spots. In order to see what you can't see for yourself, it's helpful to ask for feedback from other people. The process of identifying our blind spots can be excruciating. When you're feeling vulnerable or emotional, it's not a good time to ask for feedback. Asking for feedback in small doses and limiting each request to one aspect at a time is also recommended.

Recognize the Beliefs That Are Holding You Back

A limiting belief about ourselves and our capabilities is similar to having blind spots in our perception of the world. The fact that we are not aware of this limiting belief most of the time means that it remains hidden from us. We all, in some form or another, struggle with the limiting belief that "I'm not good enough." This self-defeating belief can put a cap on our achievements and cause us to have low expectations for ourselves. When we are young children, we are frequently exposed to a traumatic experience that forces us to make a choice regarding the kind of person we will become. This decision will become a fundamental conviction about who we are. After that, we made it our mission to either confirm or refute this belief. Your fundamental self-limiting belief manifests itself as "I'm not smart enough." Reflecting on the stories other people tell you about yourself can help you identify the limiting beliefs that you hold about yourself.

The idea that "I'm not smart enough" is one that you hold onto well into your early adult years. As you become more aware of this limiting belief, you come to the conclusion that you were trying to demonstrate that you were intelligent enough. You started college when you were 20 and graduated with a 3.2 grade point average. You believed that there was a cap on what you could achieve or become, despite the fact that you had some early success. Now, whenever your limiting belief rears its head, you have the option of choosing not to let it prevent you from moving forward. You might also be constrained by a self-limiting belief that you hold about yourself. As soon as you become aware of the belief, you are able to put in the effort to comprehend it and determine what might have been the catalyst for it. Listening to the way in which you talk to yourself can be one way to identify limiting beliefs you hold about yourself. Is there something that you consistently find fault with in your own performance? Was there a specific moment in your life when you realized that you weren't good enough? When you are able to recognize and comprehend the limiting belief that has been kept secret from you, you will be able to make significant advancements in both your professional and personal life. This is due to the fact that you now have the option to choose not to let your limiting belief prevent you from achieving your goals.

People who thrive in a competitive environment are the best candidates for leadership roles. If you are not typically competitive, you should make an effort to become so in order to build a reputation as someone who is willing to fight for what they believe to be right. Supervisors are eager to fill leadership roles with individuals whom they are confident will work hard to achieve the organization's objectives. In addition, followers are drawn to leaders who engage in healthy competition with one another because they believe such leaders have a greater chance of achieving their goals.

If at all possible, you should steer clear of direct competition in the business world. Putting into practice this strategy will enable you to keep your resources for the long haul. Having said that, there are instances in which you simply have to compete with other individuals or organizations. When you find yourself in a situation like this, you should be prepared to meet the challenge head on.

You will need to acquire the ability to compete in order to achieve the organization's goals. You instill a sense of healthy competition in your followers by modeling this quality for them and encouraging them to emulate it themselves.

You will be able to give your followers a reason to continue being persistent if you generate a sense of competition among them. You will reawaken a competitive spirit within your followers and inspire them to take the lead. They will have something to look forward to each morning, which will motivate them to get out of bed and get to work.

If you want to demonstrate your competitive spirit, try to show that you are persistent in the actions you take to reach your goals. When you or your organization are up against tough competition, that is the best time to demonstrate your competitive spirit. For instance, the majority of people would give up trying to meet their sales quotas if they were living through difficult economic times. On the other hand, a competitive leader will always be on the lookout for new approaches that can help them achieve their goals.

It's possible the leader will make an effort to break into a new market. Additionally, he or she might make use of modern technology in order to expand the number of potential customers reached. Simply having a competitive spirit is not enough to guarantee that you will do well in the role of leader in your organization. Nevertheless, this goes a long way toward motivating your followers to continue working hard toward the goals of the organization they follow.

Maintain your standing among the people you associate with.

If people stop remembering you, you won't have a reputation to protect for very long. Effective leaders steer clear of this situation at all costs by ensuring they remain relevant within their respective communities. A great number of people look down on the concept of being the focus of attention. You should make an effort to accept this role in order to ensure that the people around you will always remember you.

You need to find a way to steal the spotlight without drawing attention to yourself. For instance, make an effort to make use of your skills and the unique qualities that you possess that other people lack. Utilize your conventionally attractive appearance, for instance, as a strength in your strategy to attract people's attention. You could also use fashion to highlight and emphasize the distinctive features of your appearance.

The Struggle for Honesty, Which Is the Most Important Quality in a Leader to Have in 8

As was covered in the previous chapter, two of the most important qualities a good leader should possess are struggle and honesty. In this chapter, we are going to talk about how perseverance through adversity and the strength that comes from being honest can transform a common man into a genuine leader.

It is advised that one should fight hard for the truth, even if it appears that the entire world is working against them in their efforts to achieve it. If you are confident that whatever it is you are doing is in service of uncovering the truth, then you should not be afraid to keep up the fight. In point of fact, nobody will be able to prevent you from carrying it out, and on the other hand, everyone will gradually begin to look up to you as a leader. Even if all of your money is wasted, but you still have the courage to fight for the truth, then people will look up to you as a leader rather than a common man. It is enough for a common man to take a stand for the truth and to be the person who is able to fight for the truth while maintaining his or her integrity. Your status as a leader will become more obvious as a result of this.

Participate in the fight for integrity and the truth. Don't let anything hold you back. If during the first half of the war people see you as the person who is willing to break social norms or barriers in order to fight for the truth, you will gradually become a leader by the time the second half of the war rolls around thanks to the leadership qualities you possess. You shouldn't be restrained in any way, not even if the moon and the sun turn against you and the entire world conspires against you. It is true because if you retreat even a little bit or allow yourself to become discouraged even for a split second, it will be much harder for you to face the threats.

Struggle, Struggle, and Struggle Some More – at least until you reach a point where you can give others a glimmer of optimism in their own lives. Continue to exert yourself to the fullest extent until then. The fight for the truth is an ongoing process, and only courageous leaders have the intestinal fortitude to bear the process of fighting for the sake of the rest of the world.

A person who fights for the cause of the struggle should have muscles as strong as iron and nerves as strong as steel. This will allow them to be a leader who fights for the cause. His thought processes don't waver, and he doesn't disconnect himself from the fight for the truth. A person who is incapable of fighting for the sake of the truth will simply be referred to as a common man because he does not possess the fundamental qualities of a leader.

During the fight for truth, many people are knocked down, and a great number of others even lose their lives. But none of these things should be allowed to derail the plans of a leader. Even if only one or two of them are able to win and make a comeback, the victory will be that of the truth. Throughout the entirety of the process, those individuals who demonstrate the desire to return are the ones who will be given the title of leader. Even though he went into the fight as just another member of the populace, the fact that he prevailed there will establish him as a genuine leader. Those who are willing to fight to the end for the sake of the truth and give their lives as a martyr are also considered to be leaders because they had the bravery to give their very last drop of blood in order to see the truth triumph. It is through experiences like these that an average man can rise to the level of a leader and emerge victorious.

People are rich in the truest sense of the word when they dedicate their time, energy, and resources to improving the lives of those who are disadvantaged, destitute, and in need. We can also look at the example of laborers, who will never be mentioned by name in the annals of human history despite the fact that it is these individuals who actually carry out the work. They might appear to the average person to be nothing more than simple laborers, but in reality, these are the people who are toiling away behind the scenes to make the world a better place for everyone. They are the ones who do the work, not the educated, regardless of whether or not they can read or write. They are the ones who take on the role of leaders while maintaining the appearance of a common man. If you are one of them or know any laborers, you need to keep in mind that they are also leaders in society, keeping in mind the contribution that they have made towards their society. If you do not do this, you will be forgetting an important fact.

A leader is someone who has a deep-seated passion for the truth and places the welfare of their followers as their top priority. A leader is someone who is just like the other people in the group but has the ability to inspire and motivate them. If you are not able to pass on the passion that burns in your heart to the hearts of your fellow soldiers or comrades, then you are not contributing anything positive. You cannot be considered a genuine leader.

The source of power for those who follow a leader is the leader themselves. When a regular guy uses his good qualities to exert influence over other people and succeeds, he begins to show signs of becoming a leader over time.

For a leader, showing weakness is equivalent to taking one's own life. Therefore, a leader ought to always be powerful. It is necessary that he be the most powerful of his allies. If he is not the strongest member of the group but he is still the leader, then his status as leader is a case of "mistaken identity." He is not capable of ever being a leader. On the other hand, a leader can come from any walk of life if he has the mental fortitude to do so. One has to come to terms with the fact that weakness can only lead to slavery and not leadership.

Please don't weep in the name of the Lord. Don't blame God for the things you just can't accomplish. If you are unable to do something, it indicates that you are lacking in some way. A leader is someone who can accept responsibility for their actions, regardless of whether they have won or lost. If the average person has the ability to accept responsibility for his actions, then he is the best possible leader, or at the very least, he possesses the qualities of a good leader. Those who place blame on God for things about which they have no knowledge are part of the common man population and can never be considered leaders. A person is considered to be a leader when they are able to accept responsibility for any outcome, whether it be a victory or a loss, without feeling any shame or guilt because they are confident that they gave their all along with their teammates. A leader must always be able to take a stand for the sake of the truth and be able to destroy anything that comes in the way of withholding justice.

A genuine leader is one who reveres power and the ability to win battles. A leader venerates strength because he is aware that it is only the strength of both body and soul that can assist him in prevailing over the challenges of life and the conflict against dishonesty in order to protect the general populace.

All of the aforementioned characteristics should be exhibited by a true leader. A common man must not only adhere to them in order to become a leader, but also follow the doctrines that prescribe how to be brave enough and become bold enough to save others. This is necessary for the common man to become a leader.

Conceptions that aren't true about Loyalty

There are some beliefs that people have about loyalty that are simply wrong, incorrect, or flawed, and they can lead to problems. These beliefs can be problematic. There are times when we define loyalty by specific behaviors that are not true signs of loyalty; rather, they are true signs of something else.

One of these is acting in a manner that is excessively subservient or almost servile. There are some leaders who like to surround themselves with people who will always say "yes," also known as "brown noses." They mistakenly believe that a sign of loyalty is having followers who agree with everything that they say; however, this is not the case. Someone who is loyal to you will tell you unpleasant news when you need to hear it, but these people won't do that for you.

The idea that a follower or worker will put all of their own self-interest and motivation to the side in order to concentrate on your well-being and self-interest as a priority rather than their own is a second flawed definition of loyalty. This is not the sign of someone you can trust; rather, it is the behavior of a slave or someone who lacks self-control. A trustworthy person would never behave in this manner.

You shouldn't be looking for this kind of loyalty; instead, you should try to find someone who will work with you to achieve your goals, rather than someone who will try to imitate your worldview at the expense of their own well-being. The concept that you have to have people who will follow you even when you give them bad advice is the best way that we can describe this flaw. It is the idea that you need to have blind obedience. You can tell everyone to drink the Kool-Aid or jump off the bridge, or you can have people take actions that are simply against their self-interest simply because of blind obedience. This is where we start moving down the path from loyalty into cultishness.

When people follow you and fall into alignment with you, you know that they are aware of your decision-making process and agree with you because loyalty comes with a certain measure of intelligence and active decision-making. In other words, they are intelligent enough to follow your lead. You can have checks and balances in your team in this way, so that if you are about to lead your team off a cliff, someone else will speak up and stop you before you all fall to your deaths. This is how you can ensure that your team is safe.

It's possible that you're thinking to yourself that this section is ridiculous and that no one would ever overly serve your team, but take a moment to examine how you act in certain situations. Have there been times in your life when your followers were too obedient, and you liked it just a little bit, or when you felt a little bit like a king? If so, tell me about those times. In the course of my life, I have encountered a few of those moments, and I believe that the vast majority of other people have, as well.

There are times when you need to check and analyze your own behavior to determine whether or not you are encouraging or requiring certain behaviors. Do you expect workers to report for duty on Saturdays, despite the fact that doing so strains their connections with their families? Do you require your employees to prioritize the needs of the company over those of their families? Because of this, the team will put in extra effort because they are in need of the money, but behind your back, they are all hoping that you will suffer an early heart attack. This is not the kind of group that you want to put together, and it is most definitely not the kind of group that I want to put together.

Know Yourself as a Leader "There is always a gap between the self we think we present, and the way others see us." This is the topic of 4, which is titled "Know Yourself as a Leader."

Sheila Heen and Douglas Stone, et al.

Figure Out Where Your Blind Spots Are

Blind spots are aspects of ourselves that we do not recognize, but which are obvious to others. The effort we put into getting to know ourselves better is directly correlated to the magnitude of our personal breakthroughs and advancements in leadership. On the other hand, our insecurities and shortcomings, also known as our blind spots, can be a barrier to our achievement. Here are some examples of the questions regarding feedback that you could ask:

What do you consider to be some of my best qualities?

What do you consider to be some of my flaws?

When I'm not around, what do you think other people talk about when it comes to me?

The moment you realized that other people view you as unapproachable was a monumental turning point. You don't intend to come across as unapproachable at all. You have the desire to connect with other people and to be accepted by them. You are aware that the desire you expressed does not match the expression on your face. Because you are now aware of this fact about yourself, you are going to pay closer attention to your facial expressions and make an effort to smile, make eye contact, and acknowledge other people. You also tell your friends and coworkers that this is your default face and that they should not read anything into it. Understanding this blind spot enables you to see yourself in the world and behave in a manner that is congruent with your goals. You, too, can gain an understanding of your blind spots. In order to see what you can't see for yourself, it's helpful to ask for feedback from other people. The process of identifying our blind spots can be excruciating. When you're feeling vulnerable or emotional, it's not a good time to ask for feedback. Asking for feedback in small doses and limiting each request to one aspect at a time is also recommended.

Recognize the Beliefs That Are Holding You Back

A limiting belief about ourselves and our capabilities is similar to having blind spots in our perception of the world. The fact that we are not aware of this limiting belief most of the time means that it remains hidden from us. We all, in some form or another, struggle with the limiting belief that "I'm not good enough." This self-defeating belief can put a cap on our achievements and cause us to have low expectations for ourselves. When we are young children, we are frequently exposed to a traumatic experience that forces us to make a choice regarding the kind of person we will become. This decision will become a fundamental conviction about who we are. After that, we made it our mission to either confirm or refute this belief. Your fundamental self-limiting belief manifests itself as "I'm not smart enough." Reflecting on the stories other people tell you about yourself can help you identify the limiting beliefs that you hold about yourself.

The idea that "I'm not smart enough" is one that you hold onto well into your early adult years. As you become more aware of this limiting belief, you come to the conclusion that you were trying to demonstrate that you were intelligent enough. You started college when you were 20 and graduated with a 3.2 grade point average. You believed that there was a cap on what you could achieve or become, despite the fact that you had some early success. Now, whenever your limiting belief rears its head, you have the option of choosing not to let it prevent you from moving forward. You might also be constrained by a self-limiting belief that you hold about yourself. As soon as you become aware of the belief, you are able to put in the effort to comprehend it and determine what might have been the catalyst for it. Listening to the way in which you talk to yourself can be one way to identify limiting beliefs you hold about yourself. Is there something that you consistently find fault with in your own performance? Was there a specific moment in your life when you realized that you weren't good enough? When you are able to recognize and comprehend the limiting belief that has been kept secret from you, you will be able to make significant advancements in both your professional and personal life. This is due to the fact that you now have the option to choose not to let your limiting belief prevent you from achieving your goals.

Look for something in their answers that will help you establish a conversation. For example, if she replies, "I just like to be happy. My mom taught me to always look on the bright side," you might ask, "That's a good way to look at life. Where did you grow up?" you can say. "Maine. I'm coming home for a month and I can't wait!"

You know you're getting results from your training when someone shares personal information like this win.

S – Sympathy

Sympathy is often confused with empathy, but it is not empathy. Empathy means that we feel the same things as the child and as a result we feel sad, angry or frustrated. Instead of being a neutral facilitator and letting children come up with their own ideas; we are ourselves. This is natural for parents because our children's e motions have rubbed off on us. It can affect us when our children are sad, tired or hungry.

However, it is important that we separate our thoughts from their thoughts so that they can separate their thoughts from our thoughts. They should stand on their own feet when they are not with us. The purpose of empathy is for them to become aware of their own emotions, solve problems and find solutions. This has nothing to do with us.

"Oh, poor dear. It makes me so sad to hear that!"

"That's great! I'm so angry!" The problem you face is that showing empathy to a client who is struggling with pain will not help them at all. If you show too much sympathy to someone who is dealing with difficult emotions, they will get angry and say things like: "Wait a minute. I don't deserve mercy."

I know this from my family's experience with back pain. I don't want people to look at me with pity. When someone wants to get back to me instead of saying they're hurting too, I find comfort in knowing they actually hear me. Words about mercy make me angry.

All B.L.O.C.K.S. Although what is explained above is sometimes useful, it does not help our children recognize their emotions and find solutions. They block the flow of thought. Your children need you to listen and think so they can understand.

Slim and perfect. This white glass represents the qualities of simplicity, calmness, humility, personal fulfillment and inner peace that lead to a meaningful life. As you know, white is equal to all colors. Understand that life has its conditions. You must learn to accept reality and maintain a positive attitude in every situation in life. It is very important to be simple and humble whatever you achieve in life.

WHY HIRE INTELLECTUALLY CURIOUS RECRUITERS?

We believe heads of executive recruiting or talent acquisition should look for intellectually curious recruiters because, first, they learn faster. These people are always thinking and absorbing new information, and they are precious once you find them. Also, they fight the status quo and are always challenging old solutions, finding a better way to do something—
and they won't stop until they find it. They think it can always be done better, smarter, faster, and are not afraid of change. At the same time, they play well with others. Highly motivated employees are ge

nerally good at collaboration. They are always asking questions, looking for solutions, looking for different ways to help and solve problems. Finally, they bring knowledge. These people are really open-minded both inside and outside of work, so they never stop learning and coming up with new things and ideas. This way a lot of information will enter your organization.

How do you test intelligence? A good way to determine if someone is interested is to look for clues during the conversation. Ask curious questions. For example, ask, "Tell me something you've taught yourself in the last 6 months." Or "How did you teach yourself this new skill or idea? How did it work?" You can ask the candidate if they have questions for you: If you're getting boilerplate answers from somewhere on the internet, they're probably not the person you're looking for. If the questions you get are creative or original in some way then this is the question you need. You are trying to understand the candidate's "fix" or "growth" mindset. Ask them about the mistakes they made and how they learned from them. Ask questions like, "Tell me about a time when you had to complete a project and couldn't get all the details." The background information they provide is a good indicator of their level of curiosity. Scenario-based questions also give candidates the opportunity to prove that they are interested in asking questions or have a deep understanding of how a particular process works. Ask them how to do research when they want to learn about something they know little or nothing about. Ask other questions such as: "What book have you read recently?"; "How did you learn something new?"; "How do you strive to improve yourself?"; "Are there any skills you taught yourself?"; "What do you think about that?" What do you think about this job? make sure you're on the right side) but the recruiter can't forget to Explore and discover new things during the interview. Make candidates more curious by learning why they do what they do. Specifically, you want to identify curiosity skills and which candidates exhibit these traits. You not only want to know how they talk about their curiosity and curiosity, but you also want to know if they notice these behaviors. Some points can be found in:

· Finding challenges: Do candidates talk about situations at work when they find solutions to problems that no one else has thought of?

· Problem-solving to solve: Has the candidate explained when and how he or she has strategies for dealing with stress or difficult problems? Curious people are natural problem solvers.

• More information: Has the candidate done research on the company? It's good to hear from not only the company itself, but also from some of its competitors and the industry as a whole.

• Connect the dots: Does the candidate understand the organization's market fit and ask questions about what information you can collect in the communication and report?

•Attention: Do you feel enthusiastic and energetic when candidates talk about their interests outside of work? Passion ca n move mountains. You'll understand this better if you hug your four-year-old child. The candidate asks "why?" does he ask? Do you know your career story and future expectations? As a recruiter, you should look at candidates with the bigger picture and prioritize curiosity.

Managers often hire candidates with long-term, excellent work records, but it's also possible for these professionals to care about their own interests and fall back on the standard "playbook." Qualified candidates, regardless of job knowledge, are people who seek knowledge and try to grasp new information quickly. Leaders often work to support their teams and enable them to grow and develop. Curious people will know this for themselves. Employees want to learn, develop, improve, and grow by finding and creating new formal and informal learning opportunities by interacting with other professionals and seeking new challenges. They do not expect their employers or managers to s upport them and create opportunities for them to learn and develop. Employees who have a strong drive to better understand others, their situations, problems, and successes can bring fresh ideas and new ideas to the organization. These people never prefer to sit back and wait for the next job. They offer their leaders or managers new solutions to old and current problems. They also have many ideas on how to stay ahead of their competitors. If you're considering hiring someone from outside your industry, decision-making reliability, professionalism, and leadership may be just a few of the benefits you'll experience. Remember, people who are willing to change business are always curious, brave and not afraid of change.

Take smart risks.
Most people, including leaders, often associate uncertainty with fear and imagine worst-
case scenarios that could be even more catastrophic than they would be if they happened. When coaching a leader who is

afraid to make bold new decisions, my job is to create a safe space to explore the potential upside and downside of the options. As my clients' coach and thought partner, I can't ignore a single solution.

Building rapport and trust in relationship coaching involves telling my clients that I listen without judgment and am open to any thoughts that arise, especially those surrounded by fear and risk.

Sometimes brainstorming and developing a plan B can give the manager more confidence in case the risky option fails. In these situations, it can be helpful to consider a partner. People have more courage than they think, and I often say that the simplest definition of teaching is "support." The word "encourage" in the context of coaching means helping someone find the courage that is already there but hidden.

Current situation.

My teacher taught me to deal with situations in life, especially my job. He taught me to always tap into the sacred and infinite human imagination. The way he did it was -

no matter how much I influenced him, no matter how difficult the times, no matter how big the problem -

"What do you want to create?"

This question changed my life a lot. Life and Work. , unforgettable road. I adapted his process to work for the leaders (and others) I teach.

Tell me your current situation and I'll ask you if this is right for you. Even if you say yes, I will ask you how you can improve it. How can you make it completely different and better? What do you want to create? Why is "good enough" good enough for you? What should we do? You tell me how business is now, but I want to know how you want it to be.

Not surprising.

I once heard a successful leader tell me: "The difference between a good leader and a great leader is that a great leader tells the truth faster."

Some of the managers I work with seem to have made this purchase. A sense of power and authority by hoarding knowledge and keeping secrets that will help everyone. They may say, "I'll tell you when

I'm ready. They can't handle the truth anymore." Training leaders to move away from aggression, punishment, and judgment can build trust and respect. The same goes for creating policies for open communication and instant information sharing. One of my clients was so impressed with the results of this attitude that he hung a sign on his office whiteboard that read, "Communication solves all problems." This may not be true in every case, but setting it is enough. not surprisingly.

Use your workbook to make a list of everything you really want to learn; Do it because they love you, not because you want to or because you want to please others.

Problem #4: You don't work hard enough

As we've seen, you can't learn unless you try. It mostly means effort, work. Over the years, I have seen many people fail to achieve their educational goals because they did not study hard enough. But I have yet to see anyone fail because they did too much. Now, what I mean by "taking action" is this:

Take action on the same thing you want to learn.

The key to effective learning is to keep it simple. If you want to speak a foreign language so you can talk to a real person. If you want to be a good driver, you should actually drive.

Well understood, right?

We will discuss these tools in more detail in the effective learning tools section. < br> < br> Action steps

Using your action book, write down wha

t it means to you to take action as well as learn.

Question #5: You lack confidence in your ability to learn

Our belief in our ability to solve problems and learn everything we need to achieve our goals determines how well we learn.

Personally, I do not defend myself unless I am confident. In fact, I can clearly see that I have still been operating well below my true potential for most, if not all, of my life. The same goes for you and everyone else in the world. The important question is: Do you still see how much potential you have?

Lack of confidence in one's ability to learn can manifest as:

Not putting enough effort into learning. You don't want to be the best for fear of knowing you're not "good enough" or "smart enough." Why is your effort not enough? He is afraid of you.

Postponement. Likewise, you continue to undermine your education to avoid finding out if you are smart enough. One way to do this is to do something at the last minute that will let you off the hook if things don't turn out that way (e.g., "I could have done better if I had spent more time on this").

Actually, I'm trying to sabotage myself. I wrote less than I wanted, didn't take enough notes, avoided practicing remembering what I read, and did less research than I could have done. Fortunately, I have developed a mindset that allows me to continue my studies and long-term projects.

We will discuss in more depth how to develop positive thinking in the next section. Now, remember that you can learn most things that other people can learn. So take a moment to think about what you can and cannot learn. Focus on what you really want to learn. Remember, your happiness level is one of the most powerful learning tools you can use.

Affiliate Marketing Relationships: Same Question, Different Answers in Different Contexts Affiliate Marketing Relationships:

After a long time, Amitesh realized that h

e needed the help of a friend living in Hauz Khas. He lives in New Delhi, India. The service allowed him to stay in a rented apartment for two days to attend a two-day conference he was organizing in New Delhi. When Amitesh first asked, he received a negative response (due to a difficult conversation in his rented apartment, which he shared with four friends). He did this no matter how heavy the burden. But he didn't stop and for two days he kept trying at different times, with different thoughts, with different sounds and got the same request! And Oh My God! His friend happily agreed. How strange! Is not it? If Amitesh had not tried to convince his friend, he would not have achieved his goal. The conclusions drawn can be easily expressed as follows: Marketing and communication (in the context of business marketing) must be tested at different times and in different ways in order to make a positive difference that will lead us to achieve the desired goals. Businesses must consider and incorporate this concept of social model when engaging in any type of communication.

From a psychological perspective, the "subconscious architecture of the decision-making process" provides guidelines for decision making. Changes people make at different times when mapped by brain stimulation. When a decision is made, negative thoughts continue to flow into the brain, creating the opportunity to change the (currently made) decision, which can change if the subconscious mind changes. Once a decision is made, negative thoughts continue to flow through the mind, creating the opportunity to change the decision (that has now been made). The flow of our thoughts is actually self-monitoring, and subconscious modification is designed to reveal possible directions, including possible changes. Our hearts also think about these. It is important for companies and business organizations to deal with this concept of decision making so that they can use it as a good strategy.

A lesson for the company: "The psychology of successful communication at different times" should be internalized and us ed to amplify the company's "slogan": No negotiation is impossible. "No negotiations will be possible." The only problem is that we have to try to negotiate as planned, step by step, at different times and propose different ideas to achieve "win-win"....

Cheating during the interview: Company's personnel screening

Resume information is often presented during an interview to describe a person's personality, including personality, abilities, skills, and background. Approval ends when the individual is recognized as a "new employee" of the company. The hiring committee asks potential applicants questions based on their resumes and solicits answers from interviewers. The interview process often showcases the interviewer's personality based on the needs of the business organization. Everything written in the resume must be proven with relevant examples, experiences, certificates, similar documents, information obtained from schools and the appropriate person in the work environment. If this much is communicated pretty well, with supporting body language then, we may conclude that the interview is made right else it can be said that the interviewee is faking it. Moreover, some contact persons (in context to the contents of the resu me) should be communicated with in order to ascertain some achievements described therein. This way, we can filter out the unwanted and fake job-seekers from the talented ones. And, if not checked, the fake employees on getting into the corporate, will ruin the corporate culture as they get into the corporate with substandard qualifications and substandard organizational attributes. So, proper scanning should be done by the corporate.

Psychological viewpoint: Telling lies can be linked to generality in communications; varying over gender factor, age factor, situation, cognition level, genetic build-up, etc. There is no such thing as "cheating" in a relationship. However, in business life, we do not want employees to "negotiate". Because he will prove that he cannot do the job assigned to him. Fake employees with low skills can lead to a "weak and dysfunctional culture."

Business Training: Business organizations should always check how the recruitment process is to filter out "fake employees" in the business. In order not to allo

w the cost of the organization to retreat.
...

What is holding the team back and what is pushing the team forward?
Assessing what's holding you back and what's holding you back is the difference between creating a list of strengths and weaknesses. The list of advantages and disadvantages are costs and benefits, and these seem visible. It's often changing circumstances and stress that hold you back, whereas possibilities are what push people forward. By asking what's holding me back? What pulls me forward? Instead of defining features with their pros and cons, we ask ourselves questions that require creative answers.
Don't be afraid of limited situations, they change constantly and are usually easy to handle. They need to meet regularly. Anxiety resulting from past abuse may be deep and unsearchable. Properly defining your values can combat this as does taking the time out to brainstorm.
Do not make the mistake of holding any i

ndividual team member responsible for what may be holding back your team as a whole. At very worst you may view them as a symptom of the problem but never the cause. Their actions or any rebellious behaviour is, in all likelihood a reaction to legitimate issues that others have overlooked. Blame individual team members for team failings at your own peril, I'm a firm believer of the old adage "No man left behind".

Giving and Receiving Feedback
The feedback loop works like rocket fuel. It inspires and motivates participants beyond isolated situations into new areas. Feedback should not be reserved for performance like "teaching", it is important that most of your feedback at work is given in the form of praise, even for good or bad work. When partners know their efforts are rewarded, teamwork improves and the team is at its best.

Feedback should be an open discussion. Here are some tips to make your feedback effective.

All partners are equally important regar

dless of position or authority.

The answer should not be accusatory; this will only alienate your audience and alienate them. It's your job.

Ask people for their thoughts and opinions.

Let people speak freely. Be clear about what you want and need as a leader.

Make your presentation open-ended to allow the audience to suggest solutions.

If the feedback is about performance, it would be appropriate to use words that will be useful to the audience.

Avoid words like "you want" as they imply that past efforts were not good. Blame does not help us move forward. It demotivates people and often makes them feel less competent. Focus on patterns that lead to why events occur and root causes that can be resolved.

Equal the answers. This doesn't mean following the script and applying it to everyone. Control balance often requires constant movement and adjustment to maintain control, and control is important while providing feedback.

Group Learning

The foundation of a group's capability is organizational learning, a process by which individuals create learning that provides greater value from its source. The feedback loop created by the learning team improves the learning process exponentially. If learning alone is equivalent to learning addition and subtraction, then learning in a group or group is equivalent to learning addition and division. Or you can think of learning alone as learning to play football in the dark; Your task is to find the ball and put the candle. Group work instantly illuminates security.

Businesses, organizations and teams rely on internal information, and this information flows based on the participation of individuals in the group. New information and ideas are constantly produced due to changes. Take advantage of this constant flow of information by getting to know your team and, if possible, monitor progress by participating in activities outside of teamwork.

Developing effective training processes, a simple process that can be repeated th roughout your organization, not only saves businesses money but also gives them peace of mind that everyone is "on the same page."

When creating a learning process to train an entire team or organization, it is important to recognize that people learn in different ways. To learn more about how and why people process information differently, I recommend looking into NLP (Neuro-Linguistic Programming). Now I will talk about the basics of learning and learning styles. The four levels of learning are as follows:

Forgetfulness barrier

I don't know the sequence or the skill.

Mystery

I know the action or skill but I can't do it.

Ability to Remember

If I focus, I can do this.

Ability to forget

I can complete this task without thinking; this skill has become our second nature.

We, as human beings, are equipped with a variety of distinct methods for processing information, which are together referred to as the five senses. The fact that we prioritize certain senses over others influences the method in which we absorb information. This article will provide a concise summary of the most frequent learning styles.

People who are more visual in their learning style would rather have someone demonstrate how to accomplish a work for them, but if that is not available, visual aids such as lists, graphs, and charts can be of great assistance.

An description of the work at hand and a walkthrough of the steps necessary to finish it are frequently sufficient information for many individuals, particularly those who prefer to learn through an auditory approach.

For someone who learns best by doing, or kinaesthetically, an explanation of the skill or task at hand may be difficult to comprehend. On the other hand, demonstrating to them how the process is carried out and guiding them step by step through it would perform miracles.

What Does It Mean To Lead?

When you get a large group of people together, you'll hear a wide variety of opinions and perspectives. You frequently hear that leaders are born, and that it is impossible to develop someone into a leader. In my opinion, this approach to developing a leader is fundamentally flawed and should be avoided at all costs. For many years, those in charge of developing leaders have come from the armed forces and, to a lesser extent, businesses. I like how the United States Army defines leadership. Their definition of leadership is as follows:

"Leadership is influencing people by providing purpose, direction, and motivation while operating to accomplish the mission and improve the organization."

Get to know your guys.

Our day-to-day responsibilities instilled in us the significance of getting to know the people who reported to us as leaders. It was expected of us to have complete familiarity with our people. If I were a squad leader, it was necessary for me to be familiar with the details of the six to eight members of my squad. If I were a platoon sergeant, it was necessary for me to be familiar with the approximately sixty members of my platoon. In the event that one of my superiors questioned me about one of my employees, I was obligated to know the response to their inquiry.

We were encouraged to keep a "little Green Book" on our people's pertinent data, such as the name of their wives and children, important dates (weddings, birthdays, etc.), strengths, and weaknesses, etc.; we needed to know our people so that we could respond appropriately to these questions. In order for us to be able to answer these questions, we needed to know our people.

I discovered that by simply going through this process to get this information, I interviewed all new team members as they were assigned. As a result, I was able to quickly learn a lot about my team, even when I had a platoon of sixty people. Because of your hard work, I was able to make decisions that were not only better but also quicker and more appropriate, which ultimately led to the success of the team in achieving its objective. I was able to achieve success because I was able to maximize the success of others by capitalizing on their capabilities. I was also successful in continuing to build a stronger team by putting them through the appropriate training in order to minimize or get rid of any weaknesses we were aware of. Because of this, I was able to assist each individual in the development of the abilities they required to be successful in their careers as they prepared to take on additional responsibilities.

In a professional environment, you might not require the same level of specific information about the people you are leading, but you should still learn as much as you can about them without invading their privacy. It is especially important for you to have a solid understanding of their objectives and objectives, as well as their strengths and weaknesses. In what other ways can you assist them in achieving their goals? You would concentrate on what it takes to make them successful, and your boss would do what it takes to make sure you were successful. This would be the ideal situation.

You are only as powerful as your weakest member of the chain.

The title of this comes from an essay that was written in 1786 and published. These words remain just as relevant today as they did over two centuries ago. This indicates that there are some strong links, but there are also some weak ones, despite the fact that there are some strong links.

It's possible that some members of your team are blowing past their personal bests and exceeding expectations. Despite this, it is possible that this will be overshadowed by someone whose low number of followers is preventing overall progress. In the following chapter, you will be provided with guidance and tactics on how to improve upon those areas of weakness.

It's possible that some of the problems are your own doing. We will walk you through the steps necessary to improve them on your own. Let us get this party started.

Every member of the team is only as powerful as the team's weakest link.

Imagine that you are in charge of managing a baseball team. You are currently on a winning streak and have a very good opportunity to advance to the postseason. A more serious injury has been sustained by your team's star player than was initially believed.

Despite the fact that he has been a vital cog in the machine that has been the team's success, you have no choice but to put him on the bench. When you announce your decision and explain why you made it, the player raises objections.

"I'm good," he assures her. But you are aware that he is incorrect. You then proceed to explain to him why you are going to bench him and how playing him would actually hurt the team's chances rather than help them.

You have the final say, and you are making every effort to ensure that things do not go in an undesirable direction.

You, as the leader of the company, may be required to make challenging choices in order to maintain the continuity of the chain. However, you can be of assistance by locating the weakest links and working to strengthen them.

The process of locating the weakest link and determining how to address it

One more reason to monitor the development of your team is so that you can figure out who among them might be the weakest link. When monitoring the most important metrics, you should pay attention to who is succeeding in meeting their goals and who is falling short of those goals.

After the weak link has been identified, it is essential to have a conversation about how to address it. Inquire with them about the possible issue that has arisen. Do they fail to meet their productivity goals because they are easily sidetracked?

It's also possible that they've been in a foul mood as of late. Communicate with them in a manner that is discrete and does not cause a scene. While you are assuring them that the discussion will remain confidential, you should request that they be open and honest with you.

While you go through this process, make sure to take notes. because it has the potential to motivate you to take action to help those people. You have a responsibility to provide them with resources, including assistance from a professional, if they exhibit symptoms of a more serious condition, such as mental anguish or exhaustion.

When it comes to providing assistance to a person who might be the weakest link in the chain, every choice matters. If they are easily distracted, you should encourage them to become less easily distracted. If it is necessary, observe how they normally go about their work in order to spot any potential problems.

Participate in a call by listening in, for instance, if your team communicates with clients over the phone. Create a mental list of your thoughts and observations. You might be able to locate the source of the problem based on the monitoring you've been doing.

As soon as you have sufficient evidence, you will be able to devise a plan to fortify and improve the performance of that individual member of your team. Now, a weakness does not necessarily need to be associated with one's level of productivity. Someone might be trying to break down the cohesiveness of the team.

There is a possibility that one of the members of your team has a poor demeanor and does not get along with the other members. It is possible that you will need to take the necessary steps, one of which is terminating their employment. Because the drama in the workplace is a distraction for everyone, it's possible that you won't have time to deal with it.

A person's negative attitude may also have an effect on the relationships they have with their customers. Because of this, there is a possibility that long-term clients will take their business elsewhere as a response to one or more negative experiences they have had. And you certainly want to steer clear of this scenario.

What if you turn out to be the weakest link in the chain?

There are times when you are the weakest link. If that is the situation, it is up to you to make the adjustments that are required. Take a look at the following suggestions for food for thought:

Take better care of yourself.

Not only is it essential for every member of your team, but it is also essential for you to practice self-care. The average day at the office can be very hectic and stressful. It is imperative that you and the members of your team put the health and safety of themselves and others first at all times.

Participating in mindfulness exercises, such as deep breathing, can help reduce stress. Determine the tasks that you will complete each day. Find a good balance between your work life and your personal life that works for you.

Get rid of the feeling that you're a fraud.

You could be under the impression that you attained your position of leadership through a random series of events. It's possible that you'll feel inadequate. It's possible that you won't feel like yourself at all.

Many great leaders throughout history have suffered from the condition known as imposter syndrome. It is natural for someone in your position to have these kinds of feelings. You should make it a point to recognize the warning signs and constantly remind yourself that you are an effective leader who possesses the necessary skills.

You have arrived at this point as a result of your arduous labor, achievements, and abilities. Keep that in mind.

Get rid of the fears and beliefs that are holding you back.

This topic was thoroughly discussed in the that came before this one. Your incapacity to perform these tasks will result in the weakness of not being able to carry out the task at hand. When something like this occurs, the entire team suffers a significant loss of cohesion and becomes vulnerable to collapse.

You need to rid yourself of the limiting beliefs and fears that are holding you back, if you haven't already. Because it may result in calamity and deal a mortal blow to both your organization's team and, ultimately, its bottom line.

It is a well-known fact that a chain's overall strength is directly proportional to that of its weakest link. It takes just one of those weak links to bring down the entire team, so it is up to you to make the necessary adjustments to guarantee that everyone is on the same page and cooperating with one another.

There is a possibility that a member of your team is not being as productive as they could be, and there may be an underlying reason for this. Check that you have a complete understanding of everything that is occurring, and then devise a strategy for how the issue can be resolved. It won't be long before they've built up their strength, and the entire group will be more effective as a result.

On the other hand, you might be the weakest link. Conduct a self-evaluation, and then make the necessary changes to improve your physical and mental health in order to become a more effective leader.

The Innovative Front-Runner

A person who is able to create something from nothing is capable of exercising creative leadership. If you want to be creative, you need to have the adaptability to deal with any circumstance and the ingenuity to make use of whatever abilities and materials you have on hand.

People want to be able to rely on a leader who is creative enough to go beyond what is predictable by thinking outside the box, as there will be crucial moments along the process of building anything, and people want to rely on that leader. The innovative concepts that come from a creative leader will not only motivate other members of the team to step outside of their comfort zones and into their own creative processes, but they will also impress any member of the team who hears them.

Although the creative leader does not necessarily need to be the most creative member of the team, he or she should be forward-thinking and open-minded towards unanticipated ideas that have the potential to become very successful.

The Process of Becoming One:

Because creativity is essential to achievement, it is essential for all successful leaders to make consistent efforts to foster it. Applying these methods will set your team on the path towards innovation, so make sure everyone is on board.

Appreciate the many different types of creative expression. Because everyone on the team has the potential to be creative, you should make a habit of actively listening to their suggestions and incorporating some of them into the larger project whenever possible. Bear in mind that you do not need to be the most creative person in the group in order to be the creative leader. Rather, the creative leader is the person who is able to tap into the creative energies of all of the team members and guide this process in order to develop the greatest project possible.

Put yourself and those around you to the test. Do you believe that you have a wonderful concept in mind? Then provide evidence! Make your vision a reality and inspire others to do the same by sharing how you did it. In the event that members of a team have conflicting points of view about particular ideas, it is best to organise a civilised discussion during which everyone can share their thoughts. This will allow the more compelling points of view to emerge, while the weaker points of view can be reexamined.

Put yourself in an environment that encourages innovation. The environment that artists inhabit is rich in artistic creation. They spend a significant amount of time perusing the works of artistic greats that are housed in museums and galleries, and in order to perfect their skills, they serve as apprentices for established artists. Whatever your preferred method of creative expression may be, you should immerse yourself in it as much as possible.

You must be someone who encourages and celebrates the creative endeavours of others if you want to be a creative leader. Take cautious not to pass an overly critical judgement on the creative work of another person by contrasting it with your own concepts. Keep in mind that every single person possesses their very own one-of-a-kind style, and that if you respect that style, you will be inspiring others to have faith in their own ideas and to strive for ongoing innovation.

Honour and regard

One of the most important qualities of a leader is the ability to treat others with dignity and consideration. Therefore, cultivating respect is an essential social skill for a leader to have. Respect is a quality that can be characterised as being deferential to another person in terms of the other person's age, experience, ideas, and contributions, to name a few of these aspects. Now, let's take a look at a few of these other options.

Age.

regard for another person's age is part of the social skill set required of a leader. This regard should be shown to everyone. It is a sign that you respect youth and maturity, depending on the context, if you defer to another individual due to the fact that the other individual is older or younger than you are. You have acknowledged, in each of these scenarios, the possibility that younger people as well as elderly people may have something of worth to give. It's possible that a younger individual, who is more likely to be living in the here and now, is more knowledgeable than you are about a particular topic. And people who are more experienced than you carry with them valuable lessons that they have learned from the past and have put away in themselves. Many leaders have stated that they actively seek out the company of young people because they believe that younger people have a lot for older people to learn from them. In addition to this, those of a more senior age report that being in the company of those of a younger age helps them feel younger.

The genders.

In most cases, male persons are expected to show respect for gender norms. Respect for the members of the opposite gender is an essential social ability for men in positions of authority. Although the reasoning behind this practise is unknown, it is generally accepted among cultures all over the world. During the Middle Ages in Europe, the terms "chivalry," "gallantry," and "courtesy" were the words that were used to indicate male reverence to women. In order to recognise acts of kindness extended to women, elaborate practises came into existence. In spite of the feminist movement, which promotes the idea that men and women are equal in every way, social grace requires men to show appropriate respect to women.

Respect for women can be demonstrated in a variety of ways, such as opening doors, lifts and cars for women, allowing women to speak first, and, in some countries, allocating seats on public transportation specifically for women.

Gaining experience.

Another important social skill for leaders to cultivate is respect for those with more experience. When beginning a new project, the leader is obligated to inquire of all the individuals that will make up the project team about the specifics of each individual's prior experience in relation to the new project. It is only natural that the leader will lack all of the experience required to carry out a project in a successful manner. However, the leader must cultivate the habit of looking to the experience of others, regardless of whether they are older or younger, male or female, in order to contribute to the implementation of the project. The leader's charm as a charismatic figure is enhanced by the practise of recognising the experience of others and deferring to them. This does not in any way demonstrate the leader's lack of competence.

Perspectives and points of view.

One more key social skill for a leader to have is the ability to solicit the thoughts and perspectives of those around them. After attaining a position of leadership, whether by being elected into that position, being assigned that position, or being forced into that position, a leader is confronted with the temptation of becoming authoritarian in his dealings with the people under his charge. This can happen in a number of ways. However, a genuine leader is respectful of the ideas and viewpoints held by others. A genuine leader is self-aware enough to acknowledge that the thoughts and perspectives of others have the potential to influence the formation of his own perspectives on a topic, and consequently, the directions and instructions he provides to carry out a project.

Being humble.

An attitude of humility is the root of all the social skills that are discussed in the context of respect. Only someone who possesses a character marked by humility is capable of showing respect to another person. Therefore, cultivating humility is an essential component of a leader's social skill set. As a practise for the development of humility, Mahatma Gandhi recommended that individuals clean their own toilets on a regular basis. This was part of his profound insight. Because of this, even if one disagrees with Gandhi's views, one cannot question the humility that he possessed, which is something that helped him pave the way for others.

) The Managerial Grid (The Grid of Managers)

The inability of the traits-based approach to discern successfully between features that could differentiate successful leaders from non-successful ones resulted in a change of emphasis away from traits and towards the actions of successful leaders.

Blake and Mouton (1978) highlight two distinct forms of leadership behaviour: a) Concern for the people (also known as people-centered leadership), and b) Concern for production (also known as production-centered leadership). a) People-centered leadership:

There are some parallels to be drawn between the five managerial grids that they found and some of the leadership styles that were covered earlier. They are as follows:

1, 1Typology: This is a poor method of running a business. It is consistent with the leadership style known as laissez-faire, in which the leader does the least amount of effort necessary to get the work done. In this situation, the management does not care very much about either the employee or the production. A manager who uses this approach offers little in the way of leadership or direction to the people they supervise. He gives his subordinates more leeway to make decisions.

The 1, 9 management style, often known as the country-club management style, demonstrates how concern for output is balanced with a high one for the needs of employees or people. The manager who adopts this method demonstrates positive human relations while they are on the job. In his effort to gain social approval, he disregards the importance of being friendly.

The manager demonstrates an authoritarian leadership style known as the authority-obedience style. This is due to the fact that he is highly concerned with productivity but is less concerned with the welfare of his staff. This category includes managers who are seen as 'slave-drivers' at their places of employment. They are primarily concerned with attaining the output objective, and as a result, they push their subordinates beyond their capabilities. They have an irrational fear of falling short, and as a result, they exercise their power to make sure all of the deadlines are reached.

5, 5 Style: This is referred to as the organization's men management. It is a style that is considered to be in the middle of the road and involves striking a careful balance between concerns for production and those of the employees. The manager and others want to make sure that the production target is attained without embarrassing themselves in front of their coworkers.

9, 9 Style: This is a management style based on the concept of a team, often known as a democratic leadership style. The manager demonstrates a high level of concern for both people and production in this aspect of the media organisation; the editor and heads of unit who adopt it carry others along with them in their attempts to accomplish production targets.

Blake and Mouton found that the 9, 9 style was the most preferred since it placed a high priority on both the people and the production. The contingency theory of leadership, on the other hand, contends that the perception that there is one leadership style that is essentially superior to others is inconsistent with the concept of leadership as a result of circumstances. This position, however, provides the basis for critique.

Baby Boomers And Members Of Generation Y Are Separated By A Generational Divide.

The existing generation gap between the Generation Y and their ancestral generations, in particular the Baby Boomers, exists because of a number of reasons:

Need for Socializing

Millennials love socializing and enjoy working in groups and teams whereas the Baby Boomers and Generation X feel more comfortable when working in an individual capacity. The latter feels more work gets done when they work alone whereas the former believes that working in teams, leads to better brainstorming and an excellent exchange of ideas that breeds newer, fresher, and better approaches to completing work.

Dependency of Digital Communication and Technology

In his book, **Meet the Millennials**, Leigh Buchanon writes that the Generation Y are experts in digital communication and heavily rely on advanced technology when getting all their work done. This generation has grown up in an era where the use of internet was rising and information was instantly available. They did not have to spend hours locked in libraries and rummage through old newspapers, published journals, and books to find pieces of information because Google, Wikipedia, and other search portals were at their disposal.

On the other hand, Baby Boomers lived in a time when such advancements and conveniences were not available. They had to work hard to find things and information, which is why they were accustomed to extensive searches.

Because information is readily accessible to Millennials, they find it exciting and easy to work on unique and challenging problems. In addition, their creative abilities allow them to look for easy ways out in every situation, which is why they often look for short cuts to success.

As opposed to this, Baby Boomers faced a very tough time and had to put in extensive work to actualize their goals; this is, perhaps, one of the reason they find the approach employed by Millennials childish and believe that investing your 100 percent in a task is the only way to get it right.

The Generation Y obviously disagrees with this notion; they are of the opinion that although you need to invest hard work and time to accomplish success, some tasks can be brilliantly executed with less effort if approached cleverly.

Love Being in Charge

Millennials love being in charge of things and want their older generation to understand their need for authority. In addition, if they give an idea, they want to work on; they aspire to do things their way instead of constantly asking their baby boomers superiors for permission, authority, and consent.

In the February 2009 edition of Harvard Business Review, **Tamara Erickson** wrote an article where she stated that as a millennial, she expected to get a chance to pursue her ideas and fulfill them, and she expected her superiors, many of whom were Baby Boomers, to understand that the working models have changed; thus, they should smoothly adjust to the new working style: the millennial style of working.

Since the Baby Boomer generation grew up differently and experienced a different set of situations, they find it difficult to accept and adjust to the way Millennials work.

Crave Feedback

The Millennial employees are eager to get feedback on their performance. When they start completing a task, they expect their superiors to assess it in detail and then let them know whether they have done a good job. If they have not performed to standards, they want you to tell them how to improve instead of just being critical about their performance.

In addition, the Generation Y wants quick feedback on their work and wants their Baby Boomer or Generation X superiors to be supportive. However, the baby boomers are not accustomed to offering frequent performance appraisals and are not habitually appreciative of their employees. This explains why the millennial workers often feel dissatisfied while working for their Baby Boomer employers.

All these reasons clearly highlight why there exists a big generation gap between the Millennials and the Baby Boomers, and why the latter fails at successfully leading the former.

Now, with that out of the way, let us discuss what the Baby Boomer and Generation X employers and managers need to do to revive their relationship with the Millennials and to lead them in the best possible manner.

www.ingramcontent.com/pod-product-compliance
Lightning Source LLC
Chambersburg PA
CBHW052145110526
44591CB00012B/1863